I've Got My Wings

Poems and Short Stories That Have Shaped My Life

Jacquelyn Smithson Howard

I've Got My Wings – Poems and Short Stories That Shaped My Life

Copyright © 2015 Jacquelyn Smithson Howard

All Rights Reserved.

Cover art by Angela Moore
Prepared for Publication by Phillis Clements

No part of this book may be reproduced, stored in a retrieval system, or transmitted by any other means without the written permission of the publisher.

This book is a work of fiction and all characters are fictitious or are portrayed as fictitious. Any resemblance to persons living or dead is purely coincidental.

The information in this book is distributed on an "as is" basis without warranty. While every precaution has been taken in the preparation of this book, the author shall not have any liability to any person or entity with respect to any loss or damage caused or alleged to be caused directly or indirectly by the instructions contained in this book.

ISBN-13: 978-1512339581
ISBN-10: 151233958X

1. Inspiration
2. Poems
3. Short Stories

Dedication

I would not be who I am without the love and support of my Parents. I dedicate this book to Clarence and Abbie Smithson.

Dad, you gifted me with a thirst to dream big, treat everyone with respect, and expect to win. You let me be who I wanted to be, in the moment. You provided a safe place to grow and safely experiment with how I would handle life's curve balls throughout the many stages and experiences I would be faced with.

Mom, you gifted me with your inner strength. You exhibit such grace and peace. You gave me permission to set my bar high. You gave me the wings to fly, to be anything I choose to be. You also taught me to always be a lady. I am so blessed to have you.

I've Got My Wings

Acknowledgements

First, to my sisters, Janice and Jean, thank you for being strong and powerful women. You are loving, caring and kind. You were the first to teach me trust. You were my first barriers to the world, igniting my own path. You helped me test my boundaries and find my comfortable position, in the middle of this threesome. There are no better sisters on this planet.

To my son, Dwight, you are my gentle giant. You are the bright light in my rose-colored world. You are my peacemaker. Motherhood did not come easy for me. God's greatest gift has been loaned to me, for safe keeping. You make me proud every day.

To my love. You dance with me, through the rhythms of life. You are my Gemini twin, mirror to my soul, pillar of strength, love of my life. You gift me with your heart, and allow me to be who I am. The privilege of a lifetime is to be in the moment, with you. You have helped me fulfill this dream. I will love you always, in all ways.

To my oldest and dearest friends, Vatrice and Trisha. You are my Sister-Confidant-Prayer Warriors. You prayed for me when I couldn't pray for myself. You have always been my trusted sources. We have navigated this journey together. Thank you for always listening, laughing, and loving me through the trials of my life.

There are so many girlfriends who came late in life, for me. You know who you are. You are my coworkers, peers, teammates, travel buddies, and friends from all walks of life, all sizes, shapes, and races. All with fierce attitudes! I love you all.

I've Got My Wings

Contents

The Miracle of You 11

Lessons from the Puzzles 12

The Arch Poet 16

I Would Like To Feel Your Body.. 18

A Pleasant Visit 19

The Night of Regret 20

Birthdays 22

If You Have to Leave 23

All Closed In 24

You... 25

Smile! 26

Daddy's Canvas Story 27

Thinking 30

I Stand On Her Shoulders 32

We Stand On Their Shoulders 35

My Brave Boy! 40

Happy Birthday, from the New Kid on the Block 45

My Butterfly Love 46

Pain 48

I'm So Proud of You, my Niece 51

The Magic of Your Smile.. 53

She Spoke the Word 54

Exposed! 57

The Master Teacher 58

From Couch Potato to Full Marathon Finisher – A Lesson in Love, from my Father 62

Will You Sing to Me Too! 70

Come Back To Now 75

My Position in the Family 76

Remembering 80

A Chance Encounter 82

A Gemini Meets a Gemini 84

Parents 85

I Dreamed 87

Introduction

I started writing poems when I was 5 or 6 years old. I started like many young artists, with the "roses are red….." poems. I learned to use the poems and stories, to give voice to what I was thinking, feeling, and doing.

My Dad would read his favorite poems at the dinner table. He learned to recite them, from his Mom. My Grandmother could recite 25 or 30 verse poems without missing a word, well into her 80s and 90s.

Dad's oldest sister was my first grade teacher. She used her poems to build my foundation for always seeking knowledge. She wrote her first poetry book in her 70s.

I am a story-teller. And these pages hold some of my favorite expressions of life. I hope you will see a little of yourself in my words.

I've Got My Wings

The Miracle of You

Trust, the miracle of you, has already happened
You're here and that's a fact
Your path was magically scripted in perfect timing
You are who you are, and that's no act

You can open your heart as wide as you choose to
Open your eyes and start anew
No matter the circumstances, trials, or challenges
You know how to make it do what it do

You know every breath, every step, was choreographed
Every passenger on your path was placed
With your every need, desire, and request
All were crafted for you, with love and grace

And you may have missed the message
And temporarily stepped away
Or tried to change the path to match someone else's
And got lost along the way

But every time you wake to a brand new day
You can listen to your inner voice
Choose the bridge to burn or the bridge to cross
You have a split second to make the choice

Remember the miracle of you, it's already done
You're equipped with all you need
You can accept status quo and dream little dreams
Or you can think higher, and plant that seed

Then watch what miracles will abound for you
Where you focus, actually comes true
The world is waiting to share in the magnificent glory
Of the real miracle of you

Lessons from the Puzzles

Dad's sister was my first teacher. She used jigsaw puzzles to teach us trust, teamwork, and cooperation. Aunt Mary used poetry and rhyme to make learning fun. She used the jigsaw puzzles to teach the obvious colors and shapes, but also good habits and life lessons. Those years, in Aunt Mary's class, were the beginning of my life-long fascination with jigsaw puzzles.

I learned phonics, reading, arithmetic, colors, shapes, citizenship, and so much more from Aunt Mary and her puzzles. Long after elementary school, and all through high school, her lessons had carried me through biographies and term papers, from science to calculus and trigonometry. With each new experience, the lessons of the puzzles had emerged....what is the big picture, the end goal....where are my pieces....what is the order of progression....and without fail, the result would be successful and reveal a new level of confidence.

When my high school teacher announced that the local University was going to open a computer class to 35 students, my heart jumped. In one summer, I could be learning about the world of computer programming. All students would be tested. And the testing would be scheduled for the end of the school year, just before final exams. It was open to all of the city's high school students. You simply had to complete the request to be included. The chatter started....no girl will ever be accepted! Good grief!

As far back as I could remember, Dad spoke of the computer in my brain, and how it could only prove true, while a computer in the laboratory could be programmed to prove true or false. He said that everything you programmed into your mind's computer would cause the internal systems of your body to go to work, to prove it true. Dad was a Medic in the Army, and later, a biology teacher. He often used the computer analogy to teach us about the human body. I guessed he peaked my interest in computers as a young child.

What if I could finally get to see what Dad was talking about? What if I could make this class? I'd show those boys up, in this new coed Catholic High School. These old boys didn't want us girls here in the first place. And they already think girls can't beat 'em at anything. Yea, I might be too heavy to run or play sports, but I can rule a ping pong table or pool table until I get tired of playing. I guess working all of those puzzles gave me a sharp eye and good hand-eye coordination.

I signed up for the computer class test.

The computer class, much like the puzzles, changed the world as I knew it. The puzzles had taught me the basics of learning. <u>Hand-eye</u> coordination, which gave me the motor skills that I would need to understand computers. They taught me <u>colors & shapes</u> and <u>places & things</u> which had opened my mind to be able to imagine the impossible. The puzzles had taught me <u>discipline & patience</u>. I learned <u>to finish what I started</u>. I learned to <u>not quit</u>. I learned to <u>not give up</u> when things get too hard. I could complete the task at hand. And most importantly, I learned that everything could be solved. For me, the puzzle had to be completed. And the solution lay in figuring out the combinations to where each piece fit together.

And although Aunt Mary had planted the seeds of teamwork, partnership, and healthy competition for growth, the computer class was about to challenge it all. This was big. 35 spots with more than 15,000 student applicants.

The computer class could introduce me to how the world functioned. The world outside of the safe boundaries of my family, outside of the boundaries of my elementary and high school days. It could suddenly shift me into the fast-paced world of collaboration and competition.

The mere thought of earning a position in the class opened me. It could expose me to how things work, how businesses function, how jobs are created, products are made, and industries are built. And it was all going to be presented to me in one summer, at the most prestigious college campus in town.

My brain was excited and terrified at the same time. What if I can't grasp the concepts? What if the boys in high school were right? What if computers really are not for girls? What if…? What if…? What if…? The questions were swirling in my head and making me afraid that I would not be good enough, or smart enough, or quick enough. But the puzzle in me screamed STOP! You've got this! You know how to soak it all in, and break it into small pieces. The puzzle in me remembered that everything has a solution.

I submitted my request, studied for the exam, and received notification that I was selected and had been chosen to attend the class. That summer, I learned much more from the puzzles. I learned to trust myself in any new circumstance. I learned to never let anyone tell me what I am incapable of. And I went on to spend more than 30 years in Information Technology in some of the most aggressive Data Centers in the world.

And each computer room was darned with my favorite jigsaw puzzles. By then, I had also learned that if you put the puzzle on the table, everyone who comes to spend a few minutes searching for that specific piece, will impart some knowledge. Remember, Aunt Mary had taught that learning is so much more fun when it is shared. Programmers, analysts, operators, schedulers and managers from around the world have gifted me with an amazing education over the search for a single puzzle piece.

And on Aunt Mary's 80th birthday, it was my great honor to take her on a tour of my computer room where more than 100 of my puzzles from around the world were on display. I shared what the puzzles had taught me, and so many others, all of my life. And just like the 4 year-old in her 1st grade class, her eyes lit up as she put her hands over her heart, and then on my cheeks, as she told me how proud she was, for what I had become.

The Arch Poet

Some kids call me an "Arch Poet"
They say I write with style
They'd like to learn how to write poetry
They think the time is worthwhile

They just don't know the reality of it
It's not as easy as it seems
It takes much time and effort
It's not the product of dreams

To some it comes naturally
To others, it takes thought
For me, it's a combination
Of the situation in which I'm caught

If I'm mad, it's easy to write
The words flow naturally
If I'm happy, it takes time to write
'cause I'm too excited, you see

If I'm sad, it's not so hard
But words easily pass me by
And if I'm down, it's really hard
Because I'm wondering "why"

Poetry is the use of rhymes
Presented in a particular way
It may teach you something
Or it just might have something to say

My poetry, I think, is different
It depends upon my mood
I have to meditate for an hour
To decide what to include

I've Got My Wings

And after all my scribbling
I write the final verses
Then I read it very carefully
As one does when one rehearses

Then I dream of times ahead
When my work will be published
And suddenly, my senses return
And I think it's all cheap rubbish

It's not too fancy
But it suits me fine
My words may be simple
But at least they're mine

So they can call me "Arch Poet"
I don't mind at all
I'll keep on writing
And maybe a publisher will call

I Would Like To Feel Your Body

I would like to feel your body
Next to mine
In the still, still night
When the music is low
And the room is warm

I would like to feel your body
Warm and hot
On top of mine
To feel your heartbeat fluttering
Lustful of my body

I would like to feel your body
Stroking up and down
Harder and harder
Inside of me
Faster and faster

I would like to feel your body
Until the end of time
When together
We can begin again
And feel as one
Inside each other

A Pleasant Visit

We couldn't find a card to say
How much we think of you
For showing us a lovely time
The whole weekend through

Your southern hospitality
Is worth more than we can say
And whenever you're in our city
We hope you'll come our way

And so to just say 'thank you'
Here's our special toast to you
'Let time be ours to share
Long friendships old and new'

The Night of Regret

This has been an evening
I shall never forget
One, which I will always remember
As the 'night of regret'

It all began at work,
The night was hard and long
Nothing was in order,
And everything went wrong

I received a phone call,
Which was welcomed then
It was an invitation
To visit a 'personal' friend

Of course, I accepted,
And much to my surprise
This so called friend of mine,
Was full of childish lies

To think, I could have fallen
For this cheap excuse for a man
But luckily the truth came to light,
And now I understand

As usual, I managed quite naturally,
To get myself in this mess
But I got out in time,
Because I refused to undress

I was supposed to just 'give in'
To this poor excuse of a NUT
But I decided to turn it around,
And quietly asked 'for what?'

I've Got My Wings

I don't know what impression I gave,
Or what I might have said
But never would I consider
The possibility of going to bed

I don't care if society has changed,
Or if this is the time to be free
Before I accept the 'in crowd fads',
I'm gonna always be me

And if you don't like it, find someone new
I don't have to contend
So, I didn't, 'cause I wouldn't, and I left
And that, my friend, was the END!!

Birthdays

Birthdays are a special day
For those we dearly love
So here's a special wish for you
To let you know you're thought of

May all your dreams of today be fulfilled
May all your happy thoughts come true
May you have time to spend this day
Doing the things you want to do

You are a special person 'round here
So we'll take this time to say
Happy Birthday from the gang of us
Have a very special day

If You Have to Leave

I'd hoped this day would never come
But all good things must end
So I'd like to take this time to say
The things I've held within

This year I've spent on this job
Would never have been any fun
If people like you had never shared
The time and effort to get things done

The extra hours spent here
Would never have turned into profit
If people like you were not around
To make the best use out of it

So 'farewell and thanks' is all I'll say
And I know everyone will agree
That knowing someone as nice as you
Just fills our hearts with glee

All Closed In

Sisters get in the way of things
And I wonder if they'll ever
Decide to get away from me
And get their lives together

Husbands never understand
They want things done their way
Washing, cooking, cleaning up
So they can mess it up today

Bosses always wondering
Just why you have slacked off
They question every move you make
Just to have their chance to scoff

My goodness, what is happening?
When will it ever end?
Why should I be the butt of things?
When will I ever win?

You…..

My poetry's not the best, I guess
But it gets me over the humps
When what I try to say in words
Comes out in great big lumps

You've been there in the good times
You've been there in the bad
To know someone like you
Has made me very glad

You're that special someone
Whom I can call a friend
To talk to, just to talk to
To listen now and then

You may be gone for 6 weeks
But never gone in my heart
You're thought of very fondly
As you were from the start

Friends forever, enemies never
Is what the kids would say
So I'll just say so long, for now
Until you come back this way

Smile!

Smile!
It's a pretty big word
If you consider the fact
It determines how people watch you
And how they react

Smile!
It's always returned
In rain or shine
And anyone can do it
Even if you're handicapped or blind

Smile!
It doesn't even take a minute
For anyone to learn
And once you send it out
Watch for it to return

Smile!
It's dynamite when used correctly
And it only takes a glance
When the plan has been carried out
The glance hasn't got a chance

Smile!
Keep it up
Don't stop, for friend or foe
Never lose your ability to smile
Carry it with you wherever you go

Daddy's Canvas Story

I was about 16 years old and I was putting a jigsaw puzzle together, in my room, when my Dad came in to talk to me. I knew I must be in trouble, because Dad just doesn't usually come in to shoot the breeze. Something must be wrong. Or someone must have told him that I had done something. So I froze dead in my tracks and sat down next to him.

He said that he needed to tell me something. He said that when you are young, your life is like an artist's canvas. You don't have any idea what you will grow into, so the colors are splashed on, in vibrant colors, with no shape or order.

Everything there is familiar to you. They are your own experiences. And although the old experiences are painted over with new ones, you know what's underneath there. You know which ones to paint over, and which ones to leave in plain view. And life is fun. So your canvas is lively and free-spirited.

As you get older, your canvas will begin to take shape. The people and places will begin to take on their own order and patterns. And the colors may be subdued, but still it will be rich and vibrant. It will always show the rich ebbs and flows of your life.

I listened attentively, as my Dad painted this lovely vision of what it would be like, as I grew up. But I couldn't figure out how this was going to end, or how he was going to turn the tide and explain that this was important for me to know, in light of what he thought I had done wrong, which had brought him in my room, in the first place.

So I asked him, "Daddy, why are you telling me this?" Not that I was in a hurry to be punished, but the anticipation was killing me. He was way too calm. And I am a middle child. I was always in trouble for something. Not that I was a bad child. But I had guts and a strong temper. Anyway, all of this was going on in my head. And it seemed that time was standing still.

My Dad leaned in close to me and smiled. He said "I needed to thank you, for being a part of my canvas." He kissed me on the cheek, hugged me for a long time, and got up and walked away.

I felt 10 feet tall, in that moment. My Dad was everything to me. My Dad was my hero. And I'm not sure what he said to either of my sisters, nor did I care. He just told me that he was grateful because "I" was part of "his" canvas.

I sat for a while, thankful that I not only wasn't in trouble, but I was special. I mattered to him. And I was painted on "his" canvas. All the stars had aligned, and all was right with my world. I was my Daddy's favorite child. And I had my place on his canvas.

That story stayed with me for the rest of my life. I knew that I had always been a part of my Dad's canvas. And with the life we had, I knew my Mom and sisters were also on his canvas too. And his parents and siblings, and all of the people, places, and things that were so dear to him, were there too.

And then came a flash. I had a canvas too. And all of the people, places, and things I had done in my life, had also painted my colors bright and vibrant, and my canvas had taken on a pretty cool order and shape. I knew the crazy, silly things I had painted over since I was 16. And I was also as grateful as my Dad, for those parts of my life that had been so important, and were still in plain view.

And I still feel pretty close to 10 feet tall, knowing that I am my father's child. My canvas is rich! And over the years every time I have shared a version of this story with any family or friends, their hearts have opened, and they have allowed me to paint on their canvas.

My Dad has passed away, now 2 years ago, and I am approaching 60 in just a few months. When I see his face, I giggle still. I know that he loved me, always and in all ways.

Thinking

(A brain dump of a mixed up kid)

Thinking is a pretty big job
It takes away each thought
But once I write them down
They can never be sold or bought

Each thought is an experience
To shut out the world outside
And every time I want to think
I simply slip away and hide

I spend most of my time
Up under my bed
It's good for my thoughts
But bad on my head

Sometimes I think
That your mind should go blank
To give it a chance to rest
And refill its tank

Often, the things I think
Even I don't understand
Like sharing things
Or lending a helping hand

All my life I've struggled
To maintain something of my own
And now I base my life on sharing
As if it wasn't to own but on loan

I've Got My Wings

But things have worked out well
To have started so chaotic
It's like living a thought
That could be wild and exotic

But then I guess it is
Until something goes on the blink
So I guess I'll return
To my bedroom and think

I Stand On Her Shoulders

(Written for my Mom's 80th Birthday, which was also her Anniversary)

If you ask me today, what it means to be "Mom"
My heart would know just what to say
Because the picture that plays every day in my heart
Is of the woman we honor today

I stand on her shoulders, as proud as can be
Because she is my pillar, my rock
Her guidance and wisdom are the roots of my being
It's the place from which I take stock

You see, my Mom has an inner peace, this strength
It wraps you and makes you feel sure
I think it comes from her own Mother's life
Grandma had many challenges to endure

My Mom spent her life, with 7 brothers and sisters
And they didn't have much to speak of
But listen to the stories my Mom would tell
And you'd learn they had plenty of love

That love that my Grandma passed on to my Mom
Would be rooted and planted for me
That strength and endurance to make the best of your life
Yes, **I stand on her shoulders**, you see

It was Mom who decided she wanted to go to college
And with not one child, she entered with three
With husband and home, she finished each course
And graduated, with her teaching degree

I've Got My Wings

Now, you'd think with a husband, three children, and home
My Mom would have more than enough
But she wanted to teach, and 1st grade was her choice
And no student, in her class, was too tough

Mom taught many years, both 1st grade and 5th
With each child, she nurtured with care
It was the same with us, my sisters and me
It is Mom's values that each of us share

From Girl Scouts, to Proms, to college dorms too,
Mom has always been there
Through weddings and childbirths and yes, divorce too
Every experience she shared

Mom had in her arsenal, this reservoir that she treasures
The capacity to make you feel whole
She listened, she counseled, she laughed and she cried
And we felt safe, way down in our soul

My Mom is beauty and grace and strength and love
She is sister, wife, and Nana too
She is peace and warmth and friendship and hope
She is faithful and wholesome and true

My Mom is counselor, advisor, neighbor and friend
She is wit and will and our base
She is elegance and poise and tenderness
She is comfort and simplicity and grace

My Mom is whimsy and lyrical, free and open
She is candor and color and light
She is shelter from harm, and food for your soul
She is wisdom and structure and might

I've Got My Wings

My Mom is strength and courage and grit and purpose
She is health and wellness and worth
She is kind and gentle and squeezably soft
She is the woman who gave me birth

Yes, **I stand on her shoulders**, but let's not forget
Mom is part of a great love affair
We celebrate today, her Anniversary too
And with Dad... they're a marvelous pair

We stand on their shoulders, my sisters and me
God blessed us with only the best
God fashioned this woman and this man with His Love
And the world, is forever blessed

We love you Mom!   Happy Birthday!
We love you Dad!   Happy Anniversary!

We Stand On Their Shoulders
(Written for my Mom and Uncle on our first Family Reunion)

When Mom turned 80, I was asked to write a poem
To express what she meant to me.
"**I Stand On Her Shoulders**" was an expression, for me,
Of all of the things Mom chose to be.

This 1st Reunion is for us descendants,
To realize that our roots were great.
This poem is eventually about Mom and her siblings
Lovingly referred to as the "original eight".

Granddad was the strong silent type, I think
He worked hard for an honest day's pay
He'd come home from work and go straight to his room
And we knew that was just "his way".

From Louisville to Nashville, he rode the L&N Railroad
In the Dining Car, he was one of the Porters
It was a good job for a Black man in those days
But it was tough work, always taking orders.

Grandma, near as I can tell, didn't work outside the home
She watched us during the day
She would make sure all of the washing and ironing was done
And she would shoo us outside to play.

"G'won away from here", she'd say with a smile
"You'll get burned child, that stove is hot"
And of course we would do just as we were told
And shuffle away from that spot.

I've Got My Wings

Well, you can pretty much guess, with the 3 of us girls
In two seconds, we would be right back again
And she would realize we were playing with her
So she would shoo us away, and just grin

We had it easy, our parents were at work
And Grandma watched us whenever she could
But let's step back and acknowledge her path
Times were very different, and not always good

Remember, Mom spent her life, with 5 brothers and 2 sisters
And they didn't have much to speak of
But if you listen closely to the stories they tell
You'd know they had plenty of love

Grandma gave each one the best of herself
With whatever she had, she made due
And Granddad raised them to be good people
Yes, **We Stand On Their Shoulders**, it's true.

The first born, a son, was nicknamed 'Big Stoop'
As a young boy, he had a tall sturdy look
He worked many years at a publishing house
He was considered their chief cook

The best memories of their Christmas mornings, I'm told
Was the aroma of his biscuits, buttered and hot
While the family was busy decorating their 7 ft. tree
Those biscuits with jelly sure hit the spot

He was also quite handy with a sketch book
He drew cartoon characters, cars, and scenes
He sketched the 1950 Fleetwood Cadillac
Featured in the National Geographic magazine

I've Got My Wings

Next, was a daughter, so beautiful and tall
She had a perfect handwriting, they say!
She always had her hair, nails, and make-up done
And her clothes showed off those hips that would sway.

She worked in catering for the airlines
She was a straight A student in school,
She married her dream man and had 2 children
And those babies were their little jewels

Now, Grandma got pregnant every 2 years,
And another son came right on queue
He was nicknamed from the comic strip Lil' Abner
'Cause playing pranks was his thing to do

He never served in the military like his big brother
But he worked as a waiter at the local hotel
He married a young girl, and had 4 children
And he hung out with his friends, as well.

Boy, girl, boy, yes - my Mom, was next in line
By now the pattern was pretty clear
And although they had lots of fun together,
There was a new baby every other year

Mom often copied her sister, in hairstyle and dress,
But she also loved reading books
And of course she was barely into her teens
When my Dad set eyes on her good looks

Another son came next, and fell right into the mix
He broke the tie, in favor of the boys
He would bring 5 or 6 stray puppies home
And treat them like little cuddly toys

I've Got My Wings

He followed his big brother into the service
But the Army wasn't in his plans
So he married, and served 6 years in the Air Force,
And soon 2 children were holding his hands

It was time for a girl, the last of the daughters
She would smile and light up a room
Like her oldest sister, she worked for the airlines
And soon after, she had met her groom

By this time, there were 3 boys and 3 girls
And the siblings were born 2 years apart
Now Mom and her sister both had 3 girls
And both sets were also 2 years apart

That Uncle and Aunt moved across country to Denver
And then came their first son
I can only imagine that having 3 big sisters is tough
'Cause no battle will ever be won

Well, 2 yrs. had passed, and there wasn't a baby
The cycle was broken, and it stopped at six
The following year came news that Grandma was pregnant
And the next son was now part of the mix

He was nicknamed Porkey, not sure how that came to be
Cause these days he's so handsome and thin
And his lovely wife from Quebec is always by his side
And they now have 7 grandchildren

He followed his favorite brother into the Air Force
And traveled the world, serving 24 years
Then he worked at the post office in Maine
And retired, as another 24th year drew near.

I've Got My Wings

Well, a final 3 year itch, and Grandma was pregnant again
With 4 boys, a girl would follow the trend
But as they say, God had other plans for this family
And another son came, in the end.

With a family of eight, they were all pretty close
They played together, danced, and had fun
As we gather for this reunion, 4 generations deep
We are proud and we love each one

Yes, **We Stand On Their Shoulders**, the original eight
And they come from strong shoulders, we agree
Granddad chose Grandma as his mate
Two days before Christmas in 1923

We Stand On Their Shoulders, as strong as they taught us to be
We are educated and successful, and live near and far
Let our children and grandchildren and great-grandchildren, too
Be proud of who they are.

We Stand On Their Shoulders, let us all walk with pride
And spread the stories we've learned of each one
For this family tribute, my personal labor of love,
Well at least, this chapter is done!

My Brave Boy!

It was the summer of 1994, I think. And we were living in the South Bay of Northern California. His Dad was the Chief of Police of the State facility we were living on. In fact, his Dad had started there as the only Black Officer on the force. And within a few years, he was promoted, and became the first black Chief of Police for the State Agency. He quickly learned that his fellow officers who had treated him well as a peer, had suddenly changed their tune once he got the position a few of them had all applied for.

So, we were used to the race thing coming up in our everyday lives. I worked in the Data Center for the Department of Defense. So I was no stranger to these antics either. Anyway, understood how the game was played. We had good jobs, good family, and good friends. My son was about seven when we moved there.

He quickly learned that many of the children were not normal. This was a State facility for the Developmentally Disabled. In reality, it was a place for California's throwaways. From babies to senior citizens, those who were born with birth defects were tossed into these such facilities, and left to die. Their families never looked back. And they had become wards of the State.

But my son was a gentle soul with a kind heart. He knew the kids were special! They had special needs. They were in special circumstances. They lived in special units on the facility grounds. They had special rules. They had special attendants. They wore special helmets, or special braces, or special glasses. They talked funny, if they talked at all.

And they were all ages, colors, shapes, and cultures. And for my son, well, he spoke their language, even without words. And it didn't matter how old or how big they were. He knew they were all like children.

One thing he noticed, was that they all seemed to be happy there. So he played with them, and the other children of the staff workers for many years. He often played with his school-mates too. We lived in the big house in the back of the grounds, across from the BMX Bike track. And many nights the Police Activities League had races therefor the 6-10 year old kids. My son loved to watch the kids compete, racing around those hills and zooming past the cheering crowds.

And since Great America was close, he had a season pass for the summers. He and his friends had great fun at Great America. They could spend time unescorted by the adults, and spend a few hours hanging out and riding the rides. And he would usually come home bragging about how many times he went on the scariest rides, or what happened with one friend or another.

Now, let me be clear. This is my recollection of things, not his. He probably was not so free with the exact details of everything they did. He only told me what he wanted me to know. And he was sure I was born yesterday, and actually had no idea what they were actually doing there, or how many little girls also just happened to be there at the same time. But, it was much simpler times then, and my rose-colored glasses were in place. Besides, they were all pretty good kids.

I've Got My Wings

Well, on this day, I went to pick him up from Great America at the regular time in the same parking lot. But, my little black son was sitting on the curb with a much younger white boy, who appeared to be pretty bloodied. I could hardly get the car in gear to stop and get out. And he knew I would be frantic. So he ran toward me, with the little boy in tow, telling me that he had not done anything wrong. And the little boy was trying to catch his breath, so he could confirm that it was the truth. So, my little black son shared the following story.

"Me and my friends were leaving the park when we saw a huge crowd gathering in the parking lot. We could tell it was a fight going on, by the noises coming from there. But it wasn't my fight, so I kinda started to pass them by. But, as I got closer, I noticed that several large boys were beating up on this small kid, and no one was helping the kid.

The crowd was getting larger, and the other kids were chanting to 'hit him again'. The little boy was no match for them and I had no idea what he had done to get them so mad. But it didn't seem right that he was so outnumbered, and really outweighed.

So I stood there for a minute. Then I made my way through the crowd and told the guys that were passing the licks that 'it was enough'. The larger of the boys asked me 'what's it to you?' And I answered that 'it wasn't anything to me. I just think you have hit him enough.'"

So, my son grabbed the little guy, and walked him out of the crowd. And that was the end of his story, and why they were sitting on the curb together.

He begged me not to take him home because he wanted to stay with the little boy until his Mom came, so he would know that the older boys wouldn't circle back and mess with him again.

Now, if you are a Mom, and you heard me say earlier that we were used to the race things, you know I had a ton more questions. "How many boys were there? How old were they? Have you seen them before? Did you know them? Weren't you scared that they might start beating up on you? What were you thinking?" He shrugged his shoulders and answered each question calmly. Then he said, "Mom, it was enough!"

And I had questions for the little boy too. But I could see in his face, while my son was answering my questions that he was going to have plenty of explaining to do whenever his Mom did show up. So, we waited. I sat in the car, and my son waited on the curb, just as I had found them. And it seemed like hours had passed before his Mom showed up, and did exactly the same thing I had done, when she saw her son, bloodied, and sitting on the curb with an older black kid.

She slammed on the brakes and rushed out of that car, and her son went a-running towards her, trying to explain that "he had saved me, Mommy. Don't be mad at him. He's my friend." Before she could lay a hand on my son, I was up and out of my car, hoping this would all end well. I taught my son to be respectful. So he stayed quiet while her son answered every question she asked of him.

She listened to her son's version of the events, holding his face, and checking that nothing was broken or needed instant medical attention. Then she started to scold him about always getting in trouble and causing fights, when she realized that my son was still sort of holding on to him…and listening to the way she was talking to him.

Then she realized that I was listening too. And in that moment, it wasn't about race. It was about mothers and sons. And she could see that my son knew I would never have spoken to him like that, whether he was hurt or not. So she apologized to him, and thanked him for what he had done for her son. And she turned to me, to tell me that "I must be a good Mom, to have raised such a brave boy". She smiled and thanked us for waiting with him until she arrived. And then she scooped up her son, and drove away.

My son knew that he was my brave boy. He was my hero, for doing the right thing. And even though it could have been a very different outcome, I was proud of him. We never saw that little boy again. And I don't know if my son even thinks about it much anymore. But I do. I watched him as a caring child grow into a caring adult. He's never lost his gentle heart. And now he is a father showing his own children the way of the world. He is and always will be my brave boy!

Happy Birthday, from the New Kid on the Block

I haven't know you very long
But it's time for me to say
That you're someone special
Today and every day

I hope this day turns out to be
All that you expect
That all your dreams and goals in life
Are exactly what you get

I hope that you are happy
With whatever you decide
Because a lot of people here
Look to you as a guide

You have what most folks never get
And that's a whole lot of love
I just wanted you to know
How much you're really thought of

And, well, I guess I could go on forever
With the things I'd like to say
I wish more for you than you'll ever know
And I just wanted to say happy birthday

My Butterfly Love

(I love butterflies. They speak to the heart. This was written for someone else, for their butterfly.)

You are my butterfly
You're gentle, kind and free
Your spirit is generous and giving
And your magic is mysterious, to me

You're charming and witty
And you make me smile
Like the butterfly, you land
But only for a little while

If I reach for you too often,
You flitter and flutter away
Your true essence can't be tamed
The butterfly cannot stay

You must be admired from afar
Else your colors will fade
To hold you too close
Is like the breeze with no shade

You came to stay for only a while
And our time together is nice
We laugh and we talk
It's like sugar and spice

But, the butterfly must fly
To explore far-away lands
On the wings and a prayer
You must soar, sing, and dance

I've Got My Wings

You are my butterfly,
Come to light for just a while.
One day you will light again
And again, my heart will smile.

Pain

Don't you hate being in pain?
It sucks when things don't go right
It makes everything else suck too
And it can go on from morning to night

It makes you not want to get up
Just be numb and lie around
And hate everyone who's not in pain
Who can't recognize your frown?

What's aching you can't be explained
It's familiar and part of you
You're not ready to let go of it
And don't remember the start of it

You just know every day is the same
And nothing will ever change
And the harder you try to alter this pain
Your life seems strange

So you stay with what's comfortable
Who knows, it's really okay
This pain is your drug of choice
It's not that bad today

You actually like this pain of yours
Why change now?
Even if you could learn to let it go
You wouldn't know how

I've Got My Wings

So, no sense trying to get rid of this pain
It's such a familiar ache
Don't nobody care 'bout you anyway
You're just another mistake

But what if you can get rid of this pain?
And actually learn to feel
What if you're wrong and there really is hope?
And this pain is not real

What if you could choose to just consider
That life is good?
What if there is just a glimmer of light
Would you change if you could?

Would you hold on to this pain
So familiar and true?
Or would you start to discover
What the light could do?

Don't you just hate being in pain?
It sucks when things don't go right
So don't keep doing this same old thing
Get up and get ready to fight

Do what it takes to get rid of this pain
Stay focused and head for that light
Get away from all those people who suck
And get used to living right

It really sucks to always be in pain
And you really can't fake it
So consider what life would be like
If you really could make it

I've Got My Wings

Make it whatever you choose
It's cool to let go of the pain
It's so freeing to live to your truth
And start loving you again

I'm So Proud of You, my Niece

(Written for my niece on Illinois State election night! She won!)

I'm so proud of you
For so many things
So let me share a few
And see what the list brings

I'm proud of the little girl
Who protected family & friends
Who followed the rules
Instead of following the trends

I'm proud of the student
Who studied hard and long
To make it thru college
And emerge so very strong

I'm proud of the wife
Whose shows teamwork and heart
Your partnership stands as proof
Where your children get their start

I'm proud of the mother
You dream big and believe
You've taught your children
That they too can achieve

I'm proud of the public servant
Who stepped up, and brought it
For the Veterans and Seniors
And Students, you fought it!

I've Got My Wings

And I'm proud of the Senator
40th District, get set….
Four more years with you
Is definitely a good bet!

I love you so much!

The Magic of Your Smile

The magic of your smile
The warmth of your touch
It whispers to my heart
That this gift is just "such"

Such, designed with me in mind
Such, a moment suspended in time
Such, a gift of whimsy and joy
Such, a blessing I can call "mine"

Thank you, my love, for this "such"
This moment has filled me with joy
And, in this glorious dance we're on
I'm clapping and shouting "oh boy!"

Until I see you again…sealed with a kiss
And broadly clamoring ABSOLUTELY

She Spoke the Word

She called today
To see if I was okay
And thought of a way
For us to pray

She spoke the word
And yes, I heard

She noticed the rain
And asked again
If I had made some gain
On moving from my pain

She spoke the word
And yes, I heard

I broke my vow
I'm alone now
I didn't know how
I lowered my brow

She spoke the word
And yes, I heard

The divorce was done
The court had won
They took my son
It wasn't fun

She spoke the word
And yes, I heard

I've Got My Wings

I hurt so much
My heart, I'd clutch
I miss my son's touch
The pain's my crutch

She spoke the word
And yes, I heard

She sat awhile
And noticed the pile
An empty domicile
I lost my smile

She spoke the word
And yes, I heard

She brushed my face
And my tears erased
I felt her embrace
It was a sweet taste

She spoke the word
And yes, I heard

She asked again
How is your pain
Was the word in vain
Does the hurt remain

She spoke the word
And yes, I heard

I've Got My Wings

Then, it was swift
I felt a lift
The pain did shift
It was a gift

She spoke the word
And yes, I heard

Exposed!

I am here
Waiting with a gentle smile
To get your attention
And possibly stay awhile

I am here
To reach deep inside your heart
To help you remember
That your dreams can again start

I am here
To bring peace in your storm
To whisper, not demand
To expose your gifts, and do no harm

I am here
To share your joy, love, and peace
To empower your spirit
With things that you can release

I am here
To witness the miracle of you
To partake of the essence
Of your inner sanctum, that's true

I am here, fully exposed
And offering myself to you, whole
To trust, and to grow with
And to live out the purpose of my soul

The Master Teacher

My Aunt Mary, my Dad's oldest sister, was my first and second grade teacher. She was so patient and kind. And she introduced me to my first puzzle. She explained that puzzles not only teach you colors and shapes, but also much more important lessons that would carry me all through life.

In typical 1st grade fashion, I smiled and thought "huh". But Aunt Mary went on to explain that puzzles teach you hand-eye coordination. They teach patience and sharing, because they are fun to do alone or with a friend. And they teach you order and much more. Order is not so much the thing you do when you go to MacDonald's and tell the waitress what you want to eat. Aunt Mary was talking about the kind of **order** that meant what goes first, what goes 2nd, and so on.

Aunt Mary was so good at explaining things. She said that if I could put a 10-piece puzzle together, it would prove that I could sit still for 10 minutes. And that would be the same amount of time we would spend on some of our school work.

So, for me, 10 minutes was a long time. But it was not so bad to spend 10 minutes on math, because I liked math. And I could spend 10 minutes reading because Aunt Mary could take us to faraway lands, and we could learn about children all around the world. But 10 minutes on English or Science might not be so much fun for me, because I did not really know what they were.

Aunt Mary then gave us a 25-piece puzzle. She told us that if we could put that one together, we would get a gold star! And we would be sure to advance to the 'big kid' status.

We could sit still for 25 minutes. That was enough time to be like a good 2nd grader or even 3rd grader.

We could do a special project for our Mom on Mother's Day, or a Christmas surprise for our parents. That was a big thing. And my friends all worked hard to put our 25-piece puzzles together. And we all got gold stars.

It was fun to get gold stars from Aunt Mary, because she kept a special treat drawer. It was filled with little games and toys and some candy treats. If you got 5 gold stars in the same week, you could trade them in for a treat from that drawer.

But if you saved your gold stars, she would let you have a bigger treat for the whole class. I didn't know what that meant back then, but now I understand how much it taught me to share. I could get the treat for myself easy enough, but it turned out to be much more fun to save it for a treat for the whole class. And if you helped someone else in the class get a gold star, you got one too, for helping.

Aunt Mary was something special to me.

Since she taught me for 2 years, both 1st and 2nd grade, I've forgotten how far we got in which class. But the lessons were taught in the same way. And Aunt Mary made them fun.

If I could put a 50-piece puzzle together, I could sit longer and learn more, like the kids in middle school do. And if I could put 100-piece puzzle together, I could sit for an hour or more in a class like the high school kids do.

And if I could do a 500-piece puzzle together, I could sit in a college class for 2-3 hours at a time. And that would be really good and make me really, really smart.

Today, I can do 5000-piece puzzles and more. And I still enjoy them as much as I did when I was a child in Aunt Mary's first grade class.

And today, I manage people in countries all around the world. Today, whether you are in the United States, Canada, or the countries in South America, from Mexico and Brazil, to Venezuela, Argentina and Chile, I teach the same way Aunt Mary taught me.

If you can see the big picture, we can take the same approach each time, and be successful. Like the picture on the puzzle box, the big picture is the plan, or what we want to solution.

In class, each table worked together to put the puzzle together. So, the table would be the project team. The puzzle pieces are the steps that we need to put the plan together. And the order is which step must go first. Some projects need to have the border or rim done first. While other puzzles can be put together once each part of the picture is assembled. On the job, projects work in the same way.

Remember when you did your first big puzzle and everyone put the straight lines together. That was the outside border or rim. That showed you how big the puzzle was going to be.

It is the same today. That is what we call the "scope" of the project. Some of my projects are really big, like the 5000-piece puzzle. Some are really small, like the 100-piece puzzle.

And remember if the picture on the puzzle was of funny

bears, or dolls, or a picture of boats on the water. If you were putting it together with your friends, each one picked out the pieces from the box, to put together their part. One put the boat together, while another put the sky together. And someone else put the water together. Then, you all put your parts together to fit the whole picture together.

Today, my projects work the same way. Some teams can go off and put their part together. And the different teams are all working on their part, at the same time. Then, we all come together, and put our parts together, to make the whole project come together in the end.

It is really, really good. Just like Aunt Mary said it would be. She helped me, as a little girl, the way I help my teammates today. And I hope this tale will find its way into other elementary classrooms.

Before I close, I want to share a funny story about my Aunt Mary. Her last name was very long and hard for me to pronounce, as a first grader. And for me and my cousin, Larry, who were going to be in her class, it was much easier to call her Aunt Mary, like we had done all of our lives.

Aunt Mary explained that while we were in school, we would have to call her by her formal name, like the other kids.   And we did our best. Or so we thought.

When Aunt Mary told the story to my co-workers, when she came to visit me on my job many years later, she told the story this way:

When they came to class, I was **Mrs. C.**   And when they left school that year, there were 29 little students saying "Goodbye **Aunt Mary**. See you next year".

From Couch Potato to Full Marathon Finisher – A Lesson in Love, from my Father

This is how I came to be who I am today. Starting with my parents who married on Mom's birthday in July 1952, for my entire life, I felt like all they did was giggle and smooch. Their conversations were heart-felt and engaging. They talked *with* each other and not *at* each other. They raised us in the church, and to this day, our house is affectionately referred to as the House of Love. That's because everyone's welcome, and no one's a stranger.

Dad's mission in life was to keep Mom happy. They had what most of us dream of. An unbreakable bond, built on truth, trust, and love. Their marriage was a real partnership. Grandma once joked that they live together and work together, and even get sick together. It was true that they'd caught colds at the same time. When Mom wanted to go to college, Dad made it happen. Both of them took care of us kids, and Mom graduated with her Bachelor's Degree in Education. We lived a charmed life.

In the summer of 2004, everything changed. Just after visiting them for their Anniversary, Mom called. I knew something was wrong. She said "Honey, your Dad has had a stroke and I need you to come back home." My eyes filled with tears, and I couldn't think straight. "I was just there three days ago. Dad was fine. What do you mean he's had a STROKE?" She whispered "I don't know what happened. He's paralyzed on his right side, and I need you here."

Although I could hear the panic in her voice, I knew my Mom was strong enough to handle this. She had taken care of Grandma for eleven years, before losing her just four years earlier. She had lost both sons and most of her siblings. Mom was the pillar of strength, and we were her daughters. We would now be strong, for her.

I needed to be on the next plane, and she needed to focus all of her energy on Dad. She had enough faith to get through this. I wasn't sure if I had enough faith to match hers. I was scared. I got off the phone, cried, and prayed. You know that prayer we all pray when we want a miracle **now**. "God, I promise, if you let my Daddy get through this, I will never......" I promised God everything that night. And I was determined to make good on every word.

You can't imagine how long that plane ride was. It wasn't the direct flight, because I wanted to save the extra money, in case Mom needed it. I knew the outward face of their marriage, but the inside face was their private affair. I wasn't privy to their financial status. I knew Dad dabbled in the stock market after he'd retired. But I didn't know the net results. And this wasn't the time to ask. I had to come prepared. I learned that from him. I was successful because he taught me how to achieve success. As a young girl, I spent every spare minute by his side, listening, learning, and growing. Wherever he went, I followed him. He was my hero.

The plane landed. Mom was at the gate, and drove me directly to the hospital. Not because she knew I wanted to see Dad right away. No, she drove there, because picking me up was the only reason she left the hospital in the first place. And it was clear that she was going straight back to Dad. And she didn't care where I took that car.

They had a love affair that movies were made of. And now, her knight in shining armor was lying in a hospital bed paralyzed, with his speech slurred. For the first time in my life, I could see the fear on Mom's face. She's strong, but Dad was the breadwinner in this family. Where would the money for bills come from, without him? I didn't know if I could cover all their bills, and mine. But I would sure try hard.

The days passed slowly. Dad was determined that he would walk out of that hospital. Mom stayed by his side all day and all night. We sisters made sure she took time to eat, rest, and leave the room for small intervals. With sheer grit and determination, my Dad focused on recovering.

One day while Mom was sleeping in the chair, he said "Look at her. Isn't she beautiful? Do you know why I call her my sunshine?" I didn't remember hearing that name. But they had a language that we kids were not privy to. So I played along. "No, Dad", I answered. "Why do you call Mom Sunshine?" He turned his head and looked up at me. His face softened, and struggling with his slurred speech, he said "because when I wake, she's the first light I see!" He continued, "She is *not* going to take care of me. It is my job to take care of her. I have got to get up from here."

So, he pushed and he pulled. Masterfully using his left hand and the hospital bed rails, he maneuvered his body to the edge of the left side of the bed. For what seemed like hours, he used the automatic lifts of the bed to help him move his torso inch by inch, and then his legs, inch by inch. Soon, he'd moved and twisted his body until he was sitting up, with both legs dangling over the bed. That look in his eyes confirmed that he had every intention of keeping his promise of walking. And anyone who got in his way, was doing so at their own peril. Nothing stood in the way of my Dad taking care of my Mom.

Now, with both legs in position, using his left hand, he lowered the hospital bed until his feet were touching the floor. Using the top part of the bed, it lifted his torso until it seemed that his body would be crushed in half. Then, pulling his right shoulder with his now stronger left hand, he wedged his paralyzed side against the bed rail, and locked the rail in place. When he felt ready, he rocked until the full weight of his body was on his left leg. He was standing!

I thought he was going right over into the floor. And I reminded him that he was paralyzed. Again he rolled those eyes, in a way that all of us were quite used to, by now. He held on to the rails, standing on his own, until he was satisfied that he was in control of *his* mind and *his* body. And then he'd collapse back on to the bed. He kept this up, until he could stand, and take his first steps. Finally, being wheeled down to the front door, as it was hospital protocol, my Dad got up and walked out of that hospital, with my Mom at his side. Now, Mom had a new focus. She said that Dad had taken care of her for the first fifty years, and she was happy to take care of him for the next fifty. She handled his wheelchair like it was a toothpick. And she wielded it, with him on-board, to every follow-up appointment, every errand, and to Mass on Sunday. But, she also knew that Dad still had to do things *his* way, in *his* time. He was still the head of this household.

A few weeks after I got home, my girlfriend called to report that her grand-kids other grandmother had also had a stroke. She thought, with Dad's stroke, that we should train for a full marathon benefiting the American Stroke Association. Again, it was as if time stood still. I couldn't believe my ears. She had been my friend for many years. She was pretty health conscious. But she knew I was the complete opposite of her.

Couch Potato doesn't even come close to defining the lifestyle I had at the time. So imagine this. I was 5'8", 49 years old, and over 300 lbs. I had smoked for 30 years. I did not exercise at all. If I had to shop, and couldn't find a parking spot right in front, after circling the parking lot several times, I would drive back home, and try again another day. My diet consisted of hamburgers, fries, shakes, cakes, and every other junk food. And I had no intention of ruining any of it, with vegetables or fruits.

And this girlfriend was asking me to train for a full marathon. Using the nickname her husband had given me, she said "C'mon, Jacki Sue. We can do it together. It's in Hawaii. I'll train here, and you can train there, and we'll meet in Hawaii, girl! Say yes, Jacki Sue." I didn't even know what a *full marathon* was, so you can imagine my surprise when the word that came out of my own mouth, was "Okay." She creamed "For real? Okay Jacki Sue! We're going to Hawaii!" I hung up the phone, and sat for hours, waiting for her to call back and say that she was only teasing. But she never called back. She emailed me the forms and details for where to sign up.

In that moment, I felt God nudge me, on the couch. He reminded me that Dad had gotten up. And I felt like Dad had paid a very high price, to get *my* attention. God used Dad's stroke, to make me get up, while I still had the use of both my legs. So I got up, and I signed up. The first day, we went to a local high school, so the coaches could assess how long it would take us to complete a mile. I looked at the track and decided there was no way I could make it around that track anytime soon. My coach could already read my face. He burst that bubble quickly. "One mile", he said, "is four times around the track." With that, I proudly proclaimed to be a certified Couch Potato. He said something I will never forget. "Today, you are a FCP" My face twisted. "Today, you are a Former Couch Potato. You are now an Athlete!"

I've Got My Wings

From that day forward, I was never the same. I made every training session. And I was always the last one, or next to the last one, in. But, like Dad, with every step, I got stronger and better. After six months of training, I arrived in Kona, Hawaii to complete my first full 26.2 mile marathon. That girlfriend who had started this whole thing, had long since quit. Dad hadn't raised a quitter. I was up to the task at hand. I was now part of a 267 member American Stroke Association Team. The little town of Kona welcomed us with open arms. Although I had trained well, my coaches urged me to drop out of the full marathon, and do the half-marathon instead. They explained that with my weight, diabetes, high blood pressure, and thyroid disease, it would just be easier. With the predicted 95 degree temperature, with 95% humidity, even the best well-trained athletes will be hauled away to the medic tents. I repeated *"My Dad didn't raise a quitter.* And I have *no* intention of being the first." God must have been listening. On race day, the temperature was 82 degrees with 64% humidity, with a light sprinkle. The date, was Father's Day, 2005. Oh, what a mighty God we serve!

The buses loaded at 3:30 a.m. heading for the Start Line. I was poised to finish within the eight hour limit for Walkers. Both coaches and both team administrators were on the course. I made it to the halfway mark in just under four hours. And one coach called my parents to tell them that I'd made it halfway, and was on my way back. 13.1 miles done! 13.1 miles to go!

The light rain continued, but I didn't care because I was walking in Hawaii. No one had even considered this to be possible, for me. Everyone was praying for me to make it across this finish line. I hit mile marker 18 and noticed that the blister on my foot was forming. I was trained to redirect any negativity. So, with a slight limp, I made up silly songs. "Come on God, it's me and you! We've got a few more miles to do!"

The eight hour limit passed. The Race Director was notified that I had refused to let some stranger test my blood sugar on the course. He appeared out of nowhere, to inform me that he was forcing me off the course, for not testing. I looked up at him, rolled my eyes, and said "You will have grandchildren before you pull me off this course today!" I kept walking. He kept his distance, and walked too. Both coaches were now at my side. He relented, and said he'd hold the Finish Line open for me. With that, I proceeded toward the next mile marker.

By this time, almost all of the buses had gone past me, cheering. They'd opened the course to traffic and forced us walkers onto the sidewalk. Even the passing cars had words of encouragement. A tiny little hand appeared, flashing the Hawaiian sign for "hang loose". A small voice rang out, "you keep going 'cause we love you". She held her hand out that window until the truck was out of sight. And I got my last burst of energy.

Flanked by both coaches and both team administrators, after nine hours, I was heading into the Finish Line chute. My remaining teammates were now filling the streets, cheering me in. I couldn't speak. I was the last one to cross the Finish Line. My teammate was waiting to place the medal around my neck.

I didn't know they had held the last bus driver hostage. Someone whisked my feet into the ice buckets, and someone else handed me a banana. Afterwards, you're supposed to walk around for a little while. But they had been waiting for quite a while. Once we were all loaded on the bus, I was happy to sit for the long ride back to town. But I had to walk the length of the bus instead, to cool down. My coach called my parents again. They were both really happy. Dad replied "It's good that her name will be easy to find. It'll be at the bottom." The next day, all of the names were printed in the Kona newspaper. And I am proud to say that my name was indeed, at the bottom! To date, I've crossed 25 finish lines.

Will You Sing to Me Too!

It was January 2006, and the American Stroke Association team had arrived in Phoenix Arizona for my second marathon.

You see, Dad had a stroke in July of 2004, and I had been convinced to start training, and compete for my first full marathon at age 50. That was on Father's Day of 2005 for the American Stroke Association. Our team of 267 members was the largest to pour into the tiny town of Kona, Hawaii that year. We would compete in the marathon on part of the world famous Ironman Triathlon Course, heading through the city, out across the lava flats to Airport Highway, out to the Planetarium and back. I was the last one in that day, walking 9 hours and 25 minutes, limping across the finish line with a blister that the medics would not let me burst, due to my diabetes.

It would take 30 days to burst naturally, and not sway me from joining the team for the next training session, to compete in Phoenix where the course would take us through 3 different towns before reaching the finish line. Only this time I was not the rookie. I was a Mentor. And instead of just trying to make it in, this time, I was on a mission to make my PR. That is your Personal Record. I was going to break my 20 minute mile pace and set a new record for myself.

The team was considerably smaller, and the race was considerably larger. I had my big "mentor" mental badge on prominent display, as I strutted towards the corrals to begin the race. They announced that a Kenyan world champion was starting in the premier position, in hopes to break the world record. Well, the Runners are in the front, and Walkers are in the back. I was too far back to see him, with 33,700 people in the race. But just being in the same race…..was exciting!!!!

The guns fired and the runners were off. The corrals were shifted forward as each pace runner marking the projected finish time led the next group. Who could run 13.1 miles in 1 hour, or 2 hours, or 3 hours? Heck, I would be happy to make it in 4 hours! My finish time, in training had always been 4:20. That 20 minutes…..! Eeesh! So this was my time to concentrate and stay focused. The weather was great, so no blisters. My corral is coming up. Here I go! I feel great! There are plenty of walkers to keep me company. I made it to mile marker 1 and was making good time when I saw another teammate starting to sit down on the curb. She was new. It was her first race. And my teammate, who was her mentor, and her own husband, were at the finish line. I couldn't just leave her sitting there.

I made my way through the crowds, to get to her. I asked what was wrong and she claimed "I quit! I can't do this. My foot hurts and I want to go home."   I tried to explain that it was just nerves. "Get up. I'll walk with you for a while and you will see that it is fun. Come on!"

"Nope!" She flatly refused. "I'm not moving from this spot. You can tell my husband to come get me when you get across the finish line", she said. "Oh no, I can't leave you, and if you don't get up, I am going to sit here and sing the most awful, loud, off key, crazy songs and really annoy you

for the next 2 or 3 hours". "You've gotta get up!" I said. She didn't budge. She rolled her eyes.
And well....I grabbed her hand and pulled her to her feet, forcing her to walk with me. She cursed me for everything I was worth, because I would not let go of her hand. I pulled and sang and pulled and sang. I acted crazy, danced, and made up the most outrageous songs.

I held on to her hand for 9 miles non-stop, losing all hopes of making my PR, because I could not abandon a new teammate. It was the Girl Scout training in me, I guess. Never leave a man behind! She fussed and whined and complained the whole time. But she giggled a little too. She pleaded for me to let go of her hand. So I would let go of the left and latch on to her right hand. And she would fuss at me all over again.

Once I made it to the mile marker 10, I could see her mentor coming out to get her. When it's your first race, they come and escort you across the finish line. By the time we got close enough, she could tell that this had not been any picnic. She knew that my goal of reaching my PR was left to another race. She put her hands on my shoulder in support, and told me that she would bring her in. "Go on", she said. "I've got her. You still may have time to make your PR."

So I took off. Free of the extra weight of dragging a whole person for 9 miles, I had a new found energy level that was lighter. And my spirit was lighter too, because I had done the right thing. I had not abandoned my teammate in her time of need. I prayed that I had not contributed to any permanent damage to her foot, for dragging her 9 miles, but I had a mission in front of me. And maybe God would smile on me, for my efforts.

I skipped along for no more than a quarter mile before noticing that this woman in front of me was walking in angles from left to right. She was almost veering to one side until another walker would alert her that she was going crooked and she would correct course and veer to the opposite direction.

I approached her and asked if she was okay. I didn't know her, and she wasn't on our team. She didn't even have a race shirt from the American Stroke Association, so she was not on any of our sister teams either. She looked to be about 20 something. So, in my 50 year old mind, she would surely tell me that she was fine. And then she looked up. "Are you okay", I asked again. She turned to me and said "would you sing to me too?"

My heart sank. Who knew that anyone around me had been paying attention to my antics of the last 9 miles? I put my hand out, in support of her needing me to make up a new set of crazy songs. And that stranger and I crossed the finish line still holding hands. She introduced me to her husband who was waiting at the finish line, as the crazy singing lady who saved her out on the course from quitting.

Between her and my own teammate, I knew that my chances of breaking my 4:20 race time would only be because it would be longer...4:30, 4:40, or 4:50. But I didn't care. I had done the right thing. Well, I came across that finish line. I gulped down the ice cold water, and got my medal. My coaches and teammates came running up

to me, excited that the race results were in. "Yeah, yeah, I know I missed my time" I said. "It's okay." No, Jacki, you don't understand….your results are in. I still cry over my finish time that day. It was 3:56.
That Kenyan broke the world record by 14 seconds. And (while holding on to my finishing medal and smiling broadly) "I broke my record too."

I've never beat that PR time. But in 10 years, I have completed one full marathon (26.2 miles), one 30K (18.6 miles), and 23 half-marathons. And I still make up my crazy songs the whole way.

Come Back To Now

There is a time when the winds of change are swirling around you. It is a chance to catch the wave. And trust that there is a method to the mystery. Things that may have happened somewhere in your past, have programmed you for the moment. They flash before you like stars glittering in the nightmares of your mind.

The universe is aligning. The demons from the past are slowly finding their permanent place in hell. And the cobwebs are fading from your most recent memory. The awareness of the lessons have turned these painful memories into gifts.

You recognize the patterns, and they reveal the stepping stones of your journey. Ah….this is familiar. I've been here before. But no, I don't want to go there again! The stars are still glittering, trying to move your attention from the past, to the presence. Peace. The moment flutters away.

More stars glisten, as if a super highway is providing safe passage into a new stratosphere. Full of wonder and glory, you spring to attention, as if you can follow the path of this super highway. But it is out of reach.

Oh wait…the stars…oh, the stars are glistening. They are swirling, getting brighter, and coming closer. The fragrance is familiar. The air is crisp. The path is coming. It is still coming. Oh, it is here, all around me. The swirling….it was all for me! It is welcoming me onto this super highway. It is flowing in and through me. I can feel it. I am glittering. I am! Ahhh! Bliss! This is peace!

My Position in the Family

I am in the middle, where it is has taken me quite some time to get comfortable in. I'm not the oldest. I'm not the youngest. I'm just right, in the center. In the middle. In the core. In the heart of things. Hmmm!

This is the real power position. The vantage point from here is perfect, for me. I can see in all directions, the top, the bottom, and both sides!

My second act is coming to a close, and finally I see so much clearer these days. This will be fun to take a quick walk down memory lane and remember how I came to be in this position, in the middle. You see, I know I've changed. But I didn't know how much my parents had changed too.

Dad was right. When he married Mom and they decided to spend the rest of their lives together, they were friends first, and then lovers. They wanted the best for each other always, in all ways. I'm not sure when they decided to have a family, but they were both from large families. Dad is one of ten children. And Mom is one of eight children.

Both families lived close, and grew up together. Dad, the Lab Tech and Army Medic, and Mom had formed a bond that was so strong that over the years, other couples would model their relationships from my parent's example. Wow!

Both became teachers. And then Dad went into Sales. They were married 60 years. And shortly after their union began, Cookie was born. Mom and Dad moved into the position of parenthood. And as new Parents, they would set the foundation for the values they would instill in us. They would set the schedules and routines. They would set the parameters and boundaries for their entire environment. Cookie turned out to have Dad's medical background. She went to medical school. She is the care-giver. She is the one who can handle several things at once. She can juggle a schedule, put something on for dinner, pick up the grandkids from one spot, drop them off at another spot, get to work on time, after stopping for gasoline, and that dinner would be hot and ready when she got home. She definitely gets those skills from Mom. She is the Decider-In-Chief. And she is decisive! She got some of her decision-making skills from Dad, too. She is tough, and protective. She is strong and opinionated. But she has a heart of gold.

She asked for 2 sisters as a young child, and I guess God heard her plea, and granted her wish. I definitely danced to the beat of a different drummer. Inquisitive, stubborn, defiant, and always willing to test the waters, as I got older. Never willing to accept the status quo. Never wanting to compete, because there is nothing anyone else had that I wanted, or that I couldn't get. I am named after my Dad. I have his people skills and social acumen. I am a public speaker, teacher, and corporate trainer. I think, I too, pulled these skills from both of them.

Mom, who taught first grade, called me the Pied Piper. The kids much younger than me, would gravitate to me like bees to honey. And I had the patience to play with them for hours. Dad, who taught high school Biology, called me his analytical one. From him, I got my mathematical skills. I helped him around the house with all of his building projects and work projects. He taught me how to figure things out on my own. And I have carried those lessons throughout my life

And two years later, Cookie got her wish again, when Jean was born. The two of us, Cookie and myself, had already mastered this sibling thing, and got along pretty well, given our positions in the family. Cookie was the oldest and made the rules up as she went along. She was the first to try all of the big things in life. First in school. First at prom. First to drive. First to marry. First to have children. And I was not interested in trying to keep up with her, or follow suit. And Jean was a new commodity in the mix. Cookie knew full well how to deal with a younger sister. But I had never had this experience.

Dad explained that with Cookie, they were <u>first</u> <u>parents</u>. Everything was new and at their discretion to determine. When I came along, Dad said they were no longer new parents. They were <u>seasoned</u> <u>parents</u>, by then. There were no more surprises, and their regimens were familiar and consistent. So it was only me, who had this new experience of having a younger sister to learn how to adjust to. And I definitely struggled with a new baby in the house.

Jean was a crier. She cried about everything and seemed to never be content unless Mom was less than three inches away. And that pattern, at least in my opinion, carried into her adulthood, as she became a mother and nurtured her sons through every experience. She is their biggest cheerleader. She is Mom-In-Chief. And she followed after Dad and was the first and only one of us to get her Master's Degree.

Each of us have taken pieces and patterns from Mom and Dad, and passed them on to our children and grandchildren. And as we get older, I appreciate both of my sisters for the lessons they taught me. I appreciate the experiences we shared, with so many cousins and friends. We were Girl Scouts, and did community service. We went to the Catholic Youth Organization summer camps. We had Sunday picnics at the Lake. And we traveled every summer.

I also appreciate the lessons we didn't share also. Probably more. It was those experiences that were specially designed for me. They were uniquely crafted to make me into the woman I am today. Everything was choreographed to cross paths with hundreds of thousands of others, to teach me something new about myself. Can you imagine how many passing glances, smiles, near misses, and shared moments each of us has experienced, so far? Like pebbles on the beach they are too many to count, and so many that went unnoticed. In the grocery store, do you remember the faces? In the post office, the bank, the gas station, the car traveling alongside you in traffic, the baggage handler, and all of the social events.

Today, I think back and smile at how blessed I am, to be in the middle. I'm not the trailblazer that many first siblings had to navigate. I'm always the best worker to follow the plan, work together, and trust the outcome will yield the expected results. I'm always willing to support the younger ones, no matter their challenge. I have been blessed to always be there when I am needed the most. And from this vantage point, I get to receive blessings from all directions. The top, the bottom, and all sides!

Remembering

I grew up hanging out with the boys, not really realizing it, until I was looking backwards. The years had passed. And I was really noticing how many things I hated as a child. I hated dolls, and cooking, and dress-up, and make-up. I hated ruffles, and dresses, and girls in general, because they were wimpy and weak. They whined and complained all of the time. At least, the girls in my school seemed that way. And I was a girl. But I was tough, and brave, and not afraid of anything, except dogs!

The boys were doing fun things, riding bikes fast, building things, figuring things out. They accepted me. They trusted me. They talked to me about their issues with girls, because I was one. I was just not the type they would be interested in, in that mushy kind of way.

And so I went through life thinking I was cool. Until long after school, and long after moving away from home. Long after being separated from the boy I loved first. Long after realizing that I was stubborn and strong-willed, defiant and gutsy. Knowing that I was talented and educated, quick-witted and silver-tongued. And I liked me.

I realized that I was a loner. I was in the midst of a family unit. But I felt best when I was alone. I was never lonely. I just didn't need to be social. No one understand me. Not because of anything they did, but because I really did dance to the beat of a totally different drum.

I was a loner. And I liked being alone. I liked being with myself. I liked being lost in the mental wonderland of drifting through the planet, discovering the essence of being free. I would imagine, and float through space and time. And really, I wasn't dreaming. My eyes were open. I was really floating, in a meditative state, hovering over the world, discovering the sights and sounds, lights and smells, and colors and landscapes. I was at peace.

And I could stay in this state for hours and days, without interruption. It was innocence, and warmth. It was loving and blissful. It was grounding and comfortable. I could dance to the rhythms in my mind, and move in harmony with the ebbs and flows of some invisible highway. And I could remember how I came to be this way, remembering being nestled in my mother's womb, fighting to stay inside where it was safe. Learning later that it took 4 days of labor to get me to come out into the world. Even there, I was okay being alone. No fussing. No whining. Just an observer of all things.

Funny, looking back through the lens of all of my experiences, still I like to be alone. Still I can sit and wonder about the universe. As if guided by my own soul, showing me the marvels of the cosmos. My personal guided tour. Always feeling like, yes, I have been here before. This is familiar. This fits.

Today, is one of those days. And in the silence of this moment, life is good.

A Chance Encounter

There comes a time when our path crosses another's
And the planets seem to align
In a matter of minutes, your heart gets an impulse
To leave your comfort zone behind

A peace washes over you, in the form of a smile
And well, you can't lie
As the stranger asks about the nature of your trip
And you begin to cry

"I'm going home to see my dad
And say my final good-byes"
And the stranger leans in, and softens his voice
And I see the compassion in his eyes

"I'm sorry" he said, "Your trip will be hard,
I wish you the best, in your plight"
And in a matter of minutes, with a soft gentle hug
He parted, to catch his flight

I watched, 'til he was out of sight
And noticed the flutter within
A heart-song of some sort, giving voice to the notion
That this stranger sure feels like a friend

He's gentle and caring
And comfortable and kind
And the whole time I was home
He would pop into my mind

I've Got My Wings

Now what to do I do
With this stranger now friend
I'm too far from home
I don't know where to begin

My heart has been broken
It's so guarded and blocked
But this heart-song is stirring
A glimmer of hope has docked

It's been sealed for so long
And seared with such pain
And this stranger now friend
Made my heart feel alive again

A month has passed now
And my note, he's not returning
This pain is familiar
But this heart-song is still churning

I'll give him a call, just to thank him again
For listening, through a stranger's tears
I hope he remembers this chance encounter
And doesn't pick up on my fears

Well, the voice on the phone, is attentive
And he seems interested to meet soon
So we made plans, and this stranger now friend
Well, he has me singing a new tune.

A Gemini Meets a Gemini

(I spent time chatting earlier in the day. Then, I received a wonderful note, expressing appreciation for the good conversation, ending with 'it was a plum pleasing pleasure to meet you.')

We live and breathe and move in the world
According to the personal standards we set
Or we spend an amazingly long portion of life
Trying to analyze those things we regret

People come in and out, without thought, when we're young
When our attention button is stuck on stupid
And our dreams and wishes, and even our goals
Are trained by some crazy notions of cupid

Then, the patterns evolve and we begin to wake up
And we're grateful for the decisions we've chosen
We settle into our natural soul rhythms
And are warmed by the path that's been woven

Life is good, friends are plenty, and all is well with our hearts
And then, we settle into our own space and time
As our friendship begins, in this well-crafted cosmic collision
Just know that the plum pleasing pleasure is mine

Parents

Parents are terrific
As long as you're a child
They teach you how to live and learn
Let your imagination run wild

They teach you love and understanding
And send you off to school
To learn the basics of survival
And live by the Golden Rule

You grow up in a dream world
You've learned right from wrong
You know what's right and good
You've studied hard and long

You realize everyone has faults
Yet somehow you're to blame
Instead of wondering why you're at fault
You carry all the shame

It's time for you to graduate
You've got yourself a skill
You spent 12 years for it
Sometimes against your will

Now you're grown enough to work
Grown enough to pay the bills
But your parents still think you're a child
Brush your teeth and take your pills

Parents - will they ever see the day
When we are parents too
Or will we always be their children
In the eyes they see you through

I've Got My Wings

Will they ever retire
From being Mom and Dad
And just be plain old people
The friends you never had

Will they ever think of me
With curls and high heel shoes
Or will they always see pigtails
And little knees still bruised

I'm married now. I'm not a child.
I'm a parent just like them
But I guess that doesn't matter
I wonder if it ever will. When?

I Dreamed

I dreamed of:
Someone to make my heart sing
Someone to feel my warmth
Someone to catch me when I fall
Someone to hold my secrets
Someone to trust
Someone to talk with
Someone to dream about
Someone to expand me
Someone to take my breath away
Someone to share my dreams with
Someone to see behind my tears
Someone to see beyond my fears
Someone to see me
Someone to understand me
Someone to grow with
Someone to stand with
Someone to support my efforts
Someone to vacation with
Someone to share adventures
Someone to hold me
Someone to bless my days
Someone to dance with me
Someone to let me be me
And then I woke up in your arms, and knew that dreams
really do come true.

I've Got My Wings

I've Got My Wings

Jacquelyn Smithson Howard is a freelance writer and poet, originally from Nashville Tennessee. Her love of poetry began with her father, who recited his favorite poems at their dinner table. Her Aunt, who was her 1st and 2nd grade teacher, used poetry to make learning more fun.

Jacquelyn learned at a young age, that the poems and short stories would come without warning. She was advised to listen and write them down, no matter the time or place. She writes from her own life experiences, and shares them at family events and in other social circles.

Her father's stroke in 2004 was her wake-up call. Paralyzed on his right side, her Dad ultimately walked out of the hospital. This was a signal to get up, and at 300 lbs., Jacquelyn got moving. She completed her 26.2 mile Marathon on Father's Day 2005 in Kona, Hawaii. She has walked her way into a healthier lifestyle, losing more than 100 lbs. She has logged more than 2500 training miles, spanning 10 years, and has crossed 26 finish lines with her team, Athletes In Motion.

Jacquelyn is a member of the ZICA Literary Guild, and her poetry was published in ZICA's 3rd Anthology. She has performed her marathon story at Celebration Arts Theater, and recited her poetry at the Sacramento Poetry Center.

Jacquelyn currently lives in Elk Grove, California. She can be reached at itsmytimetosoar@gmail.com.

I've Got My Wings

Made in the USA
San Bernardino, CA
02 October 2015